ROBOZONES

ROBOT WARRIORS

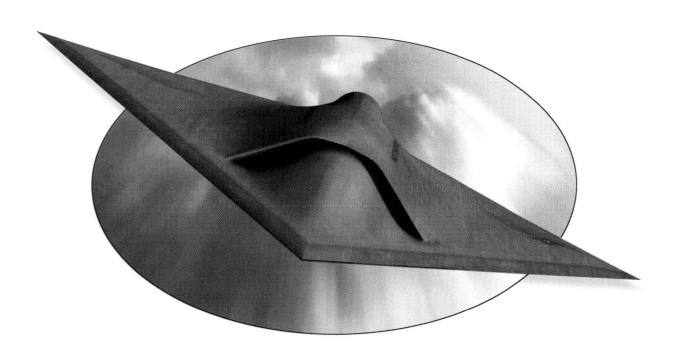

DAVID JEFFERIS

Crabtree Publishing Company
www.crabtreebooks.com

INTRODUCTION

Robot warriors help soldiers during wars, and also protect people from harm.

Like all robots today, robot warriors are computerized. They can operate on their own, or be operated by humans or by remote control.

Robot warriors often do dangerous jobs normally done by humans. Using robots for dangerous work helps prevent injury to humans.

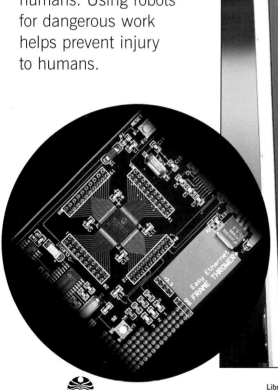

Crabtree Publishing Company
www.crabtreebooks.com

PMB 16A
350 Fifth Ave.
Ste. 3308
New York

616 Welland Ave
St. Catharines, ON
Canada
L2M 5V6

Edited by
Isabella McIntyre

Coordinating editor
Ellen Rodger

Editors
L. Michelle Nielsen, Ellen Rodger

Production coordinator
Rose Gowsell

Educational advisor
Julie Stapleton

Technical consultant
Mat Irvine FBIS

Created and produced by
David Jefferis/Buzz Books

©2007 David Jefferis/Buzz Books

Library and Archives Canada Cataloguing in Publication

Jefferis, David
    Robot warriors / David Jefferis.
(Robozones)
Includes index.
ISBN-13: 978-0-7787-2887-0 (bound)
ISBN-13: 978-0-7787-2901-3 (pbk.)
ISBN-10: 0-7787-2887-0 (bound)
ISBN-10: 0-7787-2901-X (pbk.)

    1. Robots--Juvenile literature.   2. Robotics--Military applications--
Juvenile literature.   I. Title.   II. Series.

UG450.J43 2006
j629.8'92
                        C2006-904507-0

Library of Congress Cataloging-in-Publication Data

Jefferis, David.
    Robot warriors / by David Jefferis.
    p. cm. -- (Robozones)
Includes index.
ISBN-13: 978-0-7787-2887-0 (rlb)
ISBN-10: 0-7787-2887-0 (rlb)
ISBN-13: 978-0-7787-2901-3 (pb)
ISBN-10: 0-7787-2901-X (pb)
    1. Robotics--Military applications--Juvenile literature. I. Title. II. Series.

UG450.J344 2006
623'.04--dc22
                        2006024908

Pictures on these pages, clockwise from left:
1 Electronic computer systems control a robot's actions.
2 These wastebin-sized robots are made for indoor guard duties.
3 An experimental robot submarine is being tested in a water tank.
4 This robot "eye" belongs to a ficitional combat robot that appeared in a science fiction movie.

Previous page shows:
A front view of a robot combat plane, presently in the planning stages.

CONTENTS

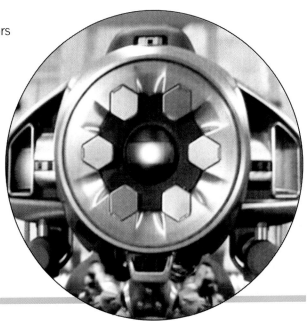

BATTLE MACHINES

The first practical robot warriors were missiles that were developed during World War II. Since computers became available in the 1960s, automated fighting machines have become important tools used in battles.

Today's robot warriors are the latest in a history of war machines that dates back hundreds of years.
1. Leonardo da Vinci drew these ideas for war machines more than 500 years ago.
2 In World War II the V-1 was a feared German missile that attacked targets in Britain.
3 Once the American Bat bomb of 1945 was dropped from an aircraft, it was steered to its target by radio signals to sink a distant enemy ship.
4 The Snark missile was used by the United States for a short time in the 1950s.

In the late 1400s, famous Italian artist and designer Leonardo da Vinci sketched ideas for a number of war machines. Among these were a mechanical, armored knight, and a chariot that had spinning knives, driven by gears as its wheels turned. He also designed a circular-shaped gun-firing battle tank. However, his ideas were far ahead of their time, and it was not until World War II that automated weapons were used in great numbers.

One of the first effective robotic weapons was the German V-1 missile, nicknamed the "buzz bomb." It was launched from a ramp and flew on a set course, before gliding down to explode.

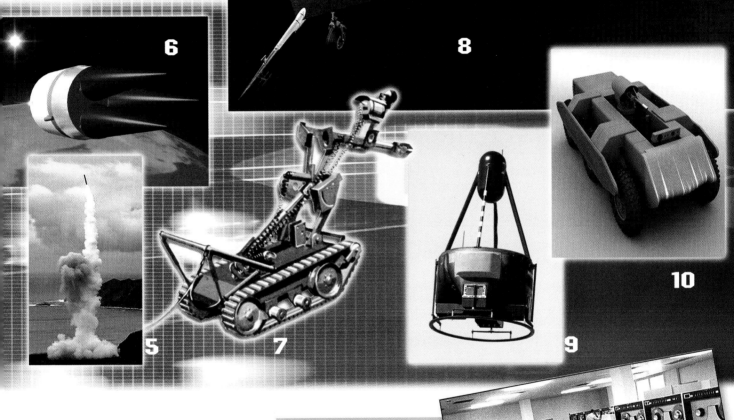

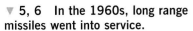 5, 6 In the 1960s, long range missiles went into service.

7 The Wheelbarrow was a robot built in the 1970s to disarm explosive devices.

8 The X-45 is an experimental robot aircraft.

9 This robot is the size of a trash can and can be launched from the back of a truck.

10 Robot ground vehicles, such as this armored scout car, are also being developed.

Computers have been the most important factor in the development of robots. Computers are the command systems that receive orders and other information, and control a robot's every function. They continue to get faster, smaller, and more powerful. More advanced computers allow robots to do difficult and complex jobs.

ROBOFACTS:
SHRINKING
COMPUTERS

The Univac III of 1961 was a powerful computer for its day, but was a massive machine taking up entire rooms. Today's laptop computers are small enough to go in a briefcase, yet are far more powerful than the Univac III. Small, lightweight computers that can process information quickly are important to robotics because they allow robots to be mobile, or move around, and perform complicated tasks.

Univac III

MacBook

SENSORS AND COMPUTERS

Computers guide a robot's actions. Sensors **allow robots to collect information from their environments using senses that are similar to human senses.**

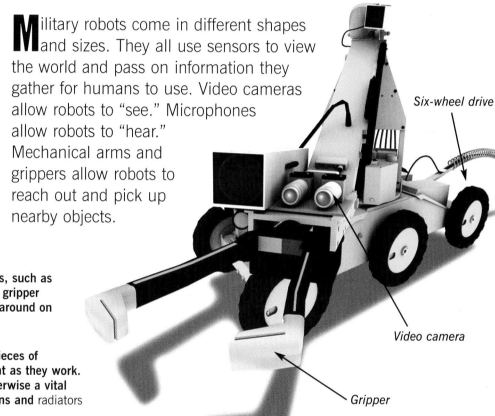

▲ **Pictures from a robot's camera are displayed on video screens. People can type instructions into a keypad to give the robot its orders.**

Military robots come in different shapes and sizes. They all use sensors to view the world and pass on information they gather for humans to use. Video cameras allow robots to "see." Microphones allow robots to "hear." Mechanical arms and grippers allow robots to reach out and pick up nearby objects.

Six-wheel drive

Video camera

Gripper

▶ **Many robots have similar sensors, such as video-camera "eyes" or mechanical gripper "hands." Most mobile robots move around on wheels or tracks.**

▼ **Computer circuits are complex pieces of machinery that produce a lot of heat as they work. Keeping them cool is essential, otherwise a vital component might melt or break. Fans and** radiators **are often used to blow heat away.**

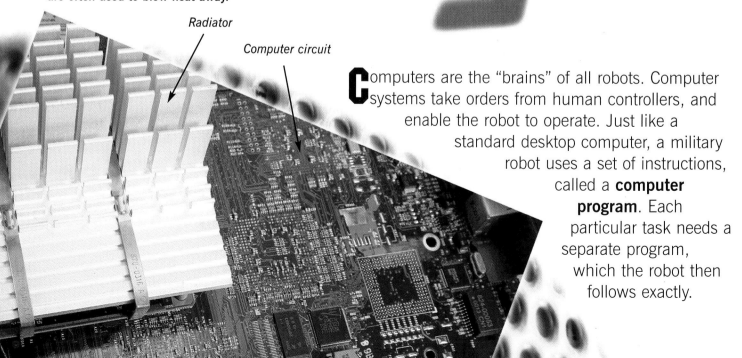

Radiator

Computer circuit

Computers are the "brains" of all robots. Computer systems take orders from human controllers, and enable the robot to operate. Just like a standard desktop computer, a military robot uses a set of instructions, called a **computer program**. Each particular task needs a separate program, which the robot then follows exactly.

◄ The Talon robot can be armed with various weapons. The Talon's operator uses a control box to guide the robot. The control box sends instructions either through a long connecting cable or by radio signals.

Robots that are guided by a human operator are currently more common than autonomous robots, or robots that can work entirely by themselves.

Skeldar robot helicopter

ROBOFACTS: COMPUTER DESIGN

Computers are used at every stage in the design of modern robot systems. Using computer simulations to model how a machine is likely to behave, or operate, means that a great deal of time can be saved during its development.

The computer simulation of a Sharc robot jet (right) shows the flow of air, shown in yellow, passing around its body. By using a simulation, designers can change and refine a robot's shape before the real thing is built. The Skeldar helicopter (far right) is another robot that has been designed using computers.

Body of aircraft shown in blue

Airflow patterns

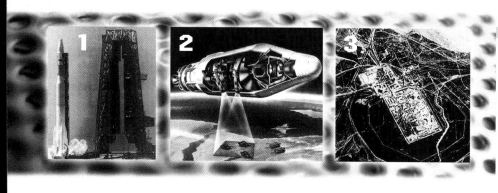

SPIES IN SPACE

The first sky spy had the code word Corona, and was launched in 1959. Since then, there have been many similar machines. After being launched into space (1), Corona (2) took pictures of the ground (3) using film cameras. The films were sent back to Earth and inspected. Today's spy satellites use digital cameras that can instantly send an image back to Earth.

The first robots used by the military were satellites. Today, "sky spies" provide the military with important information about an enemy.

Satellites are useful because they can view an area on Earth without having to launch a crewed aircraft into space. In the 1960s, piloted spy planes were shot down by missiles while on spying missions. Piloted spy planes can be captured by enemies.

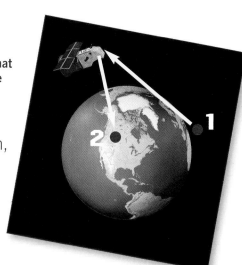

Ground antennas **send signals, including telephone and television signals, to satellites that orbit the Earth (1). The satellites then send the signals to far off locations (2).**

Satellites orbit, or revolve around, the Earth so they cannot provide a constant view of one spot. They can, however, pass over a spot several times a day. While soldiers can camouflage their weapons, or hide them in deep caves or tunnels, it is difficult to hide big military movements from spy satellites.

ROBOFACTS: SPACE IS A CROWDED PLACE!

The first satellite was sent into space by Russia in 1957. It has since been followed by thousands more, in all shapes and sizes, that do many different jobs.

Some satellites study the Earth, and send back detailed information on the weather, pollution, and other environmental concerns.

Communications satellites beam information around the world. Radio, television, Internet, and telephones all use satellites to relay information long distances.

Nobody knows exactly how many spy satellites are in space, but more than a dozen countries are now thought to use them.

Satellite sensors observe the Earth below

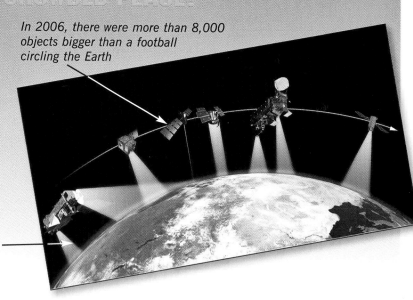

In 2006, there were more than 8,000 objects bigger than a football circling the Earth

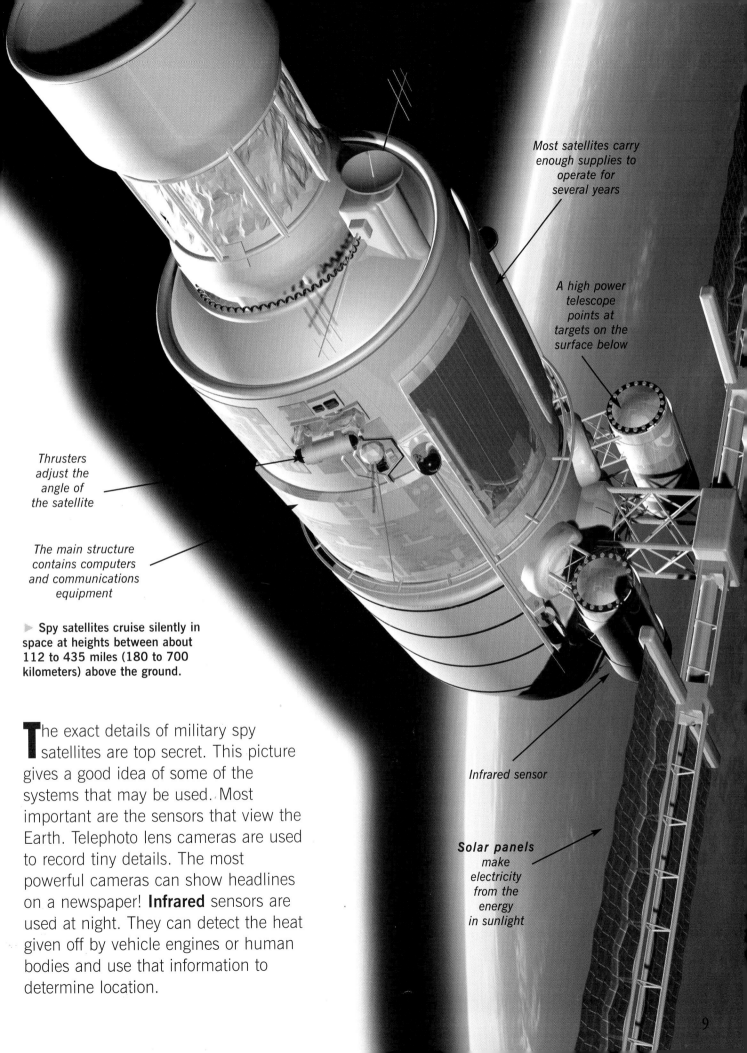

Most satellites carry enough supplies to operate for several years

A high power telescope points at targets on the surface below

Thrusters adjust the angle of the satellite

The main structure contains computers and communications equipment

▶ Spy satellites cruise silently in space at heights between about 112 to 435 miles (180 to 700 kilometers) above the ground.

Infrared sensor

Solar panels make electricity from the energy in sunlight

The exact details of military spy satellites are top secret. This picture gives a good idea of some of the systems that may be used. Most important are the sensors that view the Earth. Telephoto lens cameras are used to record tiny details. The most powerful cameras can show headlines on a newspaper! **Infrared** sensors are used at night. They can detect the heat given off by vehicle engines or human bodies and use that information to determine location.

▲ An iStar spy plane ready for launch from a robot truck.

EYES IN THE AIR

Reconnaissance **missions usually involve soldiers traveling over dangerous territory, collecting information about their enemies. Robot planes can go on these missions without risking soldiers' lives.**

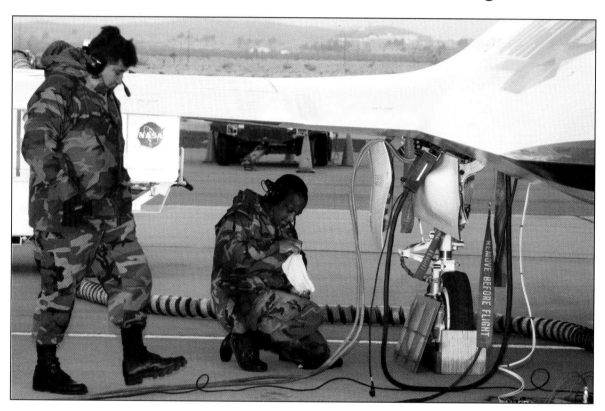

◄ **Robot planes may not have humans aboard, but maintenance and refueling is still done by people. Here, technicians connect vital supplies before the flight of an experimental robot plane.**

Space satellites are good for long-range overhead views, but for close-ups, other solutions are needed. This is when robotic airplanes called **UAVs**, or Uncrewed Air Vehicles, are useful.

The smallest UAVs are no bigger than a model airplane. Powered by a small and very quiet motor, a UAV can be sent over enemy territory, where it flies unseen and unheard. The UAV's operator flies it by remote control. Pictures of the enemy's territory are taken by an onboard camera, and are seen on video screens by military personnel. If a UAV is shot down, no pilot will be killed or captured.

◄ **There are many different kinds of photo-spy planes, ranging from tiny hand-launched types, to bigger machines that need a launching ramp for takeoff.**

ROBOFACTS: INSIDE A ROBOT

The Global Hawk's hump nose holds a satellite antenna, used to exchange information with space satellites. The plane has long, glider-like wings that enable it to cruise very high, out of range of enemy missiles. Its single jet engine gives the plane a speed of up to 404 miles per hour (650 kilometers per hour).

The biggest UAV spy plane is the Global Hawk. It is an autonomous robot, which means it operates on its own, following orders that are programmed into its computers before the flight. Military personnel monitor the flight and can change the spy plane's mission if needed. The Global Hawk can fly for up to 36 hours before needing to refuel, and can cruise up to 12 miles (20 kilometers) above the ground.

Satellite antenna

Jet engine

Sensor bay

UCAVS IN ACTION

The latest robot planes not only collect information about enemies, but also carry out attacks. They are called UCAVs, or Uncrewed Combat Air Vehicles.

▲ A Predator UCAV is put into a crate for transport to a combat zone.

▶ This UCAV is prepared for a dawn takeoff.

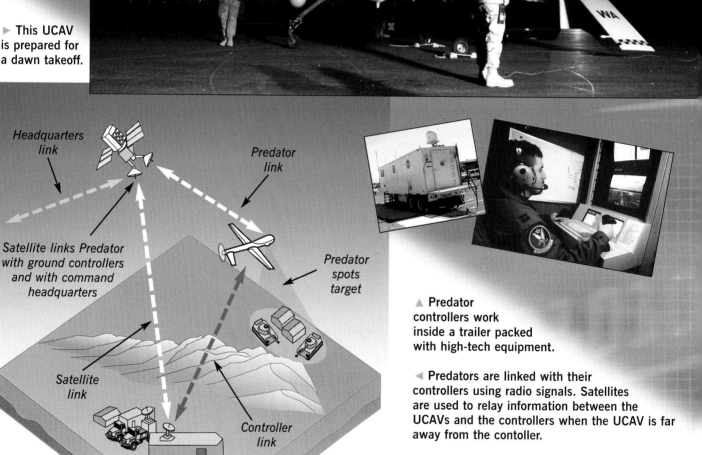

Headquarters link

Predator link

Satellite links Predator with ground controllers and with command headquarters

Predator spots target

Satellite link

Controller link

Ground controllers and their equipment

▲ Predator controllers work inside a trailer packed with high-tech equipment.

◀ Predators are linked with their controllers using radio signals. Satellites are used to relay information between the UCAVs and the controllers when the UCAV is far away from the contoller.

Among the most widely used UCAVs is the Predator, an American-built aircraft just 27 feet (8 meters) long. First designed as a spy plane, the Predator has since been armed with missiles under its wings, and has made many successful attacks in war zones. Like other small robot planes, the Predator often surprises enemy forces because it is too small and quiet to be spotted easily.

ROBOFACTS: SHARC AND NEURON

Uncrewed Combat Air Vehicles are evolving. Among the aircraft companies working on a new generation of UCAVs is Saab of Sweden, better known for its well-designed cars.

The bright yellow Sharc is an experimental jet designed to test fully autonomous flying. The Sharc has proven successful in test flights but will need a few design changes.

On one flight, it used up almost the entire runway before coming to a stop.

Saab is using what they have learned while developing the Sharc to design a new jet UCAV, called the Neuron. The Neuron is designed for "stealth" flights, using high-tech materials and a special shape to make it nearly invisible to the electronic sensors of enemy defenses.

Sharc experimental UCAV

Neuron stealth UCAV

Other countries have copied the Predator's design. Military planners around the world see the useful features of these UCAVs. They are cheaper to make and to fly than aircraft flown by human pilots, and if a UCAV is shot down, there are no casualties, and no need for dangerous rescue missions.

◀ Predators have a belly dome (circle at left) with cameras, radar, and heat detectors. These allow a Predator to spot targets during the day or night and through cloud or mist. Missiles (circle at right) are mounted under the wings.

▲ The Nanoseeker microsub should be almost undetectable by enemy forces. Its sensors are carried in the fingernail-sized nose section.

ROBOTS AT SEA

Air forces are not the only department in a country's armed services that can use robots. Many naval forces use robots at sea.

Many duties performed by a naval force do not involve fighting. Navy vessels patrol waters and search for lost ships. Both are ideal jobs for robots.

Submarines are usually large and expensive to build, packed with weapons and crew. The Nanoseeker is an experimental robo-sub little bigger than a finger, and powered by a tiny electric motor. The Nanoseeker could one day be used to spy on enemy ships, cruising undetected through enemy waters.

The Fire Scout robot helicopter can fly patrols up to 124 miles (200 kilometers) from its home ship. When armed with homing torpedos, the Fire Scout will be able to hit targets, much like the Predator UCAV can.

◄ The Fire Scout was developed as a robotic version of an existing helicopter, the Schweizer 333. Fire Scout can fly from most ships, even small ones.

ROBOFACTS: SEARCH AND RESCUE

The Navy uses robots for search and rescue missions, as well as for combat.

The Super Scorpio is a robot that can dive deep under water. It is controlled by humans aboard ship, through a long cable.

The Super Scorpio uses electric motors to move around. It is also equipped with video cameras to provide pictures, and metal arms that can grip objects under water. The Super Scorpio is useful for finding sunken ships and helping in rescue operations.

This Super Scorpio is being prepared for launch. It will be swung over the side of this naval ship by a powerful crane

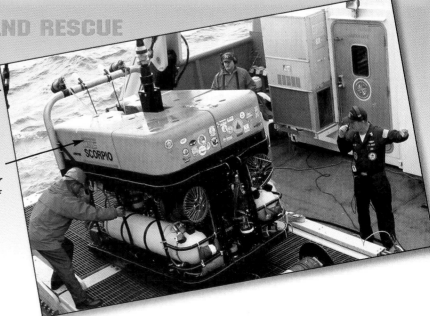

The Robo-Lobster's "claws" could be used as sensors for detecting mines

▲ Robo-Lobsters are experimental robots that walk like real lobsters. They could be used to find undersea mines.

▶ The Robo-Lamprey was built to test new kinds of propulsion. Instead of using a propeller, it lashes its tail from side to side.

Super Scorpio is steered using hand controls

A diver makes sure that the robot is working properly

A murky video view of a sunken wreck

ROBOT ARMY

Robotic systems already help combat troops work better and more safely. Soon, robots may completely take over many dangerous combat roles.

▲ Swords robots come in several versions. These robots cost about $125,000 each, which sounds like a lot of money, but is considered good value for a modern weapons system.

A Swords robot rolls off a cargo plane's ramp, ready for action

Introducing robots to the world's armies is big business. Many countries, including the United States, plan on spending a lot of money on military robots. Leading the way are robots called **Swords**, or Special Weapons Observation Reconnaissance Detection Systems. Swords can be refitted for different missions, and are able to operate in snow and ice, or heat and dust. Swords can tow loads of up to 200 pounds (90 kilograms).

◀ Features of a Swords robot include the operator control unit (1), which includes a video screen and radio antenna. The robot can carry up to seven cameras, including one on the mast (2). Tracks (3) give the robot grip when moving across rough ground.

▼ This armored robotic patrol vehicle has wheels that move up and down to allow it to keep going on very rough terrain.

Other robots being developed include fast patrol vehicles. The patrol vehicle above will be able to travel across almost any rough ground, and follow a target all by itself. It has wheels, which allow it to reach higher speeds than tracks.

▲ If an explosion flips over this robot vehicle, its six wheels swing over to allow it to keep going even when upside down.

ROBOFACTS: ROBOTS LEAD THE WAY

The picture on the right shows a robot and soldiers working together in a practice session. With a top speed of just over five miles per hour (eight kilometers per hour) a Swords robot can keep up with a jogging soldier.

Swords robots are tough, too. In battle, one Swords robot was blown off the roof of a carrier truck by enemy gunfire. The truck was crossing a bridge at the time, and the robot plunged into the river far below. Despite being damaged, the robot was recovered. With some minor repairs, the robot was soon back in action.

SUPERSOLDIERS

The latest robotic equipment helps soldiers perform their jobs better.

▲ A robot soldier in the future could look something like this machine from the 2000 movie, *Red Planet*. In the film, the robot carried out various missions, from patrols to combat.

Robots do not feel hunger or fear, or forget information. According to some experts, robots will eventually be better fighters than humans, but not for many years. For now, robots are best at helping soldiers.

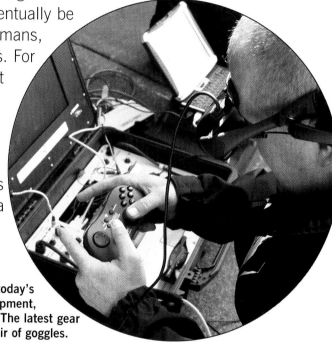

Robots can act as "force multipliers," which is anything that helps soldiers perform with better efficiency. For example, a squad of troops that uses a UAV spy plane gets information instantly. Using a robot plane is quicker and cheaper than having a human pilot do the same job.

▶ Robotic systems are standard issue for many of today's soldiers. Robots are controlled using command equipment, including laptop computers and hand-control units. The latest gear includes a miniaturized video display worn like a pair of goggles.

ROBOFACTS: IS BIGDOG A SOLDIER'S BEST FRIEND?

BigDog carries up to four Army backpacks

BigDog is an experimental robot built to carry heavy loads for soldiers. BigDog is well named, as it is about the same size as a Great Dane. It can move along at over three miles per hour (five kilometers per hour), climb steep slopes, and carry 120 pounds (55 kilograms) – all this over ground that is too rough for wheeled or tracked vehicles.

BigDog has a steel body with an engine that powers a hydraulic system, a computer, and a measurement unit that tracks its movement and position. Each metal leg has sensors that work with the measurement unit to check where the legs have to be, in order to keep BigDog upright and moving in the right direction.

At present, BigDog is remote-controlled, but future versions will be able to run themselves. They will also be able to run faster and carry twice as much. These advanced BigDogs should be ready for carrying duties around the year 2015.

The Bleex 1 exoskeleton (left) will be replaced by a final version (right) that will let a soldier carry a 200 pound (90 kilogram) pack.

Design for a possible future robot fighting machine

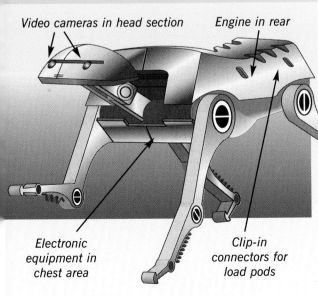

Video cameras in head section

Engine in rear

Electronic equipment in chest area

Clip-in connectors for load pods

▲ The BigDog load-carrier will include these features when it is ready for military work.

A robotic suit is being developed that acts as an **exoskeleton**, giving its wearer extra strength. The Bleex exo-system is an experimental design that allows its wearer to easily carry heavy loads.

Bleex 1 has two powered leg braces, dozens of electronic sensors, a control computer, and a small gasoline engine for power. The plastic and **carbon fiber** braces are linked to a pair of standard army boots. No commands are needed to use the braces – they simply follow the wearer's foot movements. Bleex 1 weighs about 100 pounds (45 kilograms) and allows a soldier to carry a load of 70 pounds (32 kilograms). To the soldier, the entire load feels like it weighs only five pounds (two kilograms)!

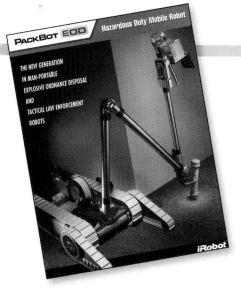

PACKBOT EOD — Hazardous Duty Mobile Robot

THE NEW GENERATION IN MAN-PORTABLE EXPLOSIVE ORDNANCE DISPOSAL AND TACTICAL LAW ENFORCEMENT ROBOTS

iRobot

▲ This is the maker's brochure for Packbot, a robot with a long, multi-jointed arm. The arm can reach around corners and into tight spots, which makes it useful for dealing with UXBs that have been hidden in awkward places.

DANGER – UXB!

One of the most useful jobs that a robot can do is to clear deadly minefields and help deal with UXBs, or unexploded bombs.

Working with unexploded bombs, or **UXBs**, is a very dangerous job. This used to be a task for the military, who had to disarm, or make safe, UXBs that had been left by the enemy. Today, police officers must also deal with UXBs. Suspicious packages sometimes show up in buildings, on public transportation, or even through the mail. Police treat these as possible UXBs.

▲ Here are three robots that deal with UXBs. Some bomb-disposal robots can even climb stairs.

Small robots are ideal for dealing with bombs. A robot equipped with cameras can approach a UXB, allowing police or soldiers to see the UXB while staying a safe distance away.

ROBOFACTS: HUNTING FOR DEADLY MINES

Mines are among the world's deadliest weapons. Most of their victims are ordinary people who live in war zones. Many mines are left in the ground after a battle, making an area dangerous for many years after.

Robots are now starting to be used for clearing minefields, making life less dangerous for all, especially the bomb squads.

One of the most advanced robots is the crab-like Ariel, an experimental machine specially built to work in shallow water and on beaches.

Laying mines is quick, but digging them up is very dangerous

Ariel moves slowly and silently, much like a crab.

◄ ▲ **British forces were among the first to use robots for UXB work. Here, a suspicious package is taken away for safe disposal.**

▼ **Fetch is a robot, made in the United States, that can hunt for dangerous objects. Here it looks for a UXB hidden under leaves.**

There are various ways to deal with a suspicious package. One way is to have a robot pick up the package and take it very carefully to a safe place where the bomb can be set off without hurting anyone. It is certainly safer for the bomb disposal crew, as they can be away from the explosion.

ROBOCOPS

Robotic systems are working hard in our cities, helping keep crime off the streets.

▲ The movie *Robocop* made the idea of a robotic police officer popular. Robocop is a cyborg, a blend of human and machine systems.

Robots like the movie character Robocop are not likely to be created in the near future, but simpler robots are already helping the police. Typical jobs include guarding, and more recently, police have followed the military by using UAVs for air patrols.

In Los Angeles, police put their first UAV, called the SkySeer, into the air in June 2006. SkySeer has low-light and infrared cameras and can cruise for up to an hour at 23 miles per hour (37 kilometers per hour). The small aircraft backs up the crewed helicopters that patrol the skies, by helping search for missing children or lost hikers. The SkySeer can also help spot burglary suspects on rooftops and follow suspects fleeing on foot.

The SkySeer weighs only three pounds (1.5 kilograms)

▼ Robot expert Phil Bennet (right) discusses an Andros 5A robot with two policemen from Albuquerque, New Mexico. The robot has helped them deal with suspicious packages since 2000.

▲ Robart III is an experimental robot built to carry out a wide range of security research.

▲ Security cameras have been used for many years. The latest robotic video-eyes use advanced pattern recognition systems to spot unusual things in a crowd.

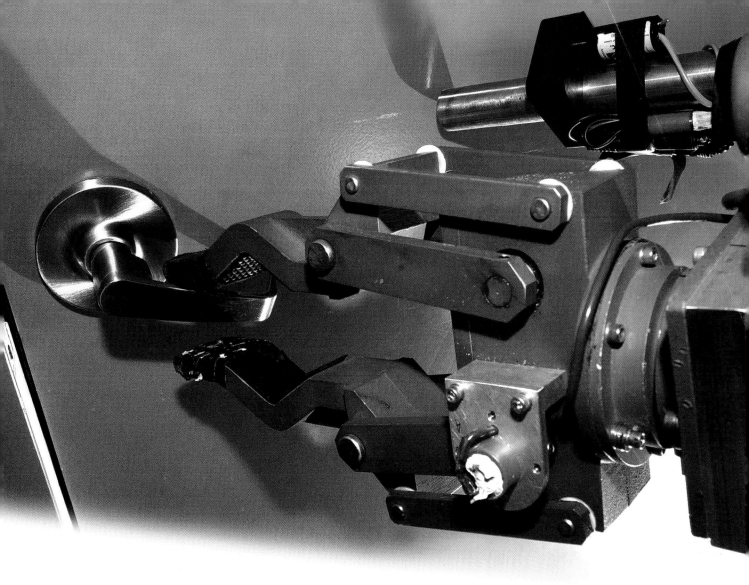

▲ Robot grippers need to move smoothly. Here, a door is opened gently in case an explosive on the other side is set off by a bump.

Robots are a useful tool for gaining access to areas where lethal gases, chemicals, or explosives are stored. The picture above shows a tough, metal robotic gripper designed for such work.

ROBOFACTS: THE FIRST ROBOCOP?

Long before there were real robots, people imagined them and what they could be used for. A robocop character was created for a story in *Science and Invention* magazine in 1924.

This early robocop, shown at right on the cover of *Science and Invention*, moved using tank-like tracks, and was controlled by police using radio signals. Devised as a riot-control system, it had some special equipment, including hands that could whirl lead weights, and a loudspeaker so loud that it could temporarily deafen rioters!

This popular magazine was published in 1924

HOME GUARDS

Robot technology is helping to make our homes safer with systems that watch for intruders and alert the police or security companies.

Personal robots in our homes have so far been limited by their large sizes, heavy weights, and high prices. Today, manufacturers are able to make smaller sized robots and their prices are continuing to drop, making them more practical and affordable for home owners.

Among a new wave of smaller and simpler robots is the little Nuvo from Japan. Nuvo is just 15 inches (39 centimeters) tall and has only 15 electric motors to move, about half the number used by other similar robots. While Nuvo is not cheap, it is less expensive than many earlier robots, and costs are likely to drop as more are sold.

▲ The Room Blaster robot is sold as a toy guard that fires soft rubber disks, when intruders set off its sensor alarm. The Room Blaster may be a toy, but its technology is advanced enough to be used for real-life defense machines.

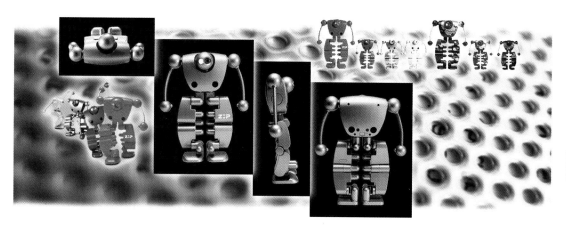

◀ The Nuvo robot was the first to come in a range of designer colors and finishes, aimed at fashion-conscious buyers.

Nuvo can do several jobs, such as acting as a security device. Nuvo can send pictures to a cellular phone over the Internet, allowing owners to check in on their homes.

Other makers of security robots include the Fraunhofer company of Germany. Its machines are used in shops, museums, and at big public events.

▶ Fraunhofer Watchrobots are often used as night guards. Similar robots, with tracks instead of wheels, were used for security at a number of soccer stadiums in 2006.

Rubber wheels allow the Watchrobot to glide quietly around a guard zone

◀ A home computer keeps this robohome safe from intruders. Sensors keep a regular check on movements in the house.

▶ Roborior is a small video watchdog that sends pictures to a home owner's cellular phone.

Homes of the near future will have robotic security systems built in, just as today's houses come with plumbing and electricity.

▶ This home-security robot uses sensors to avoid bumping into people or furniture.

ROBOFACTS: SPOT THE THIEF

Robots and cellular phones are becoming useful tools for guarding homes. The blue robot (above right) patrols the home, and can send out an alert to the home owner's phone if anything unusual occurs, such as an intruder, a water leak, or even a house fire.

The robot's alert comes as a video message, allowing the home owner to decide whether or not emergency services need to be contacted.

Video message shows an intruder about to steal a robot vacuum cleaner

Robot video camera lens

25

▲ This is a design idea for a future robocop, with legs for patrolling streets. Pop-out wheels could unfold to enable it to chase a stolen vehicle at high speed.

THINGS TO COME?

In the future, robot warriors will take over jobs now done by humans. Having robots do dangerous jobs will save human lives.

Cities of the future may be safer if robot police officers are used. Robots could work with human police officers to catch criminals.

▲ Could robots one day turn on their human creators? The frightening possibility was explored in a 1984 movie, called *The Terminator*.

Shown on the next page is a design for a future robot police officer. Its looks are based on a robot in the movie *Robocop*. Its systems are real, based on research being carried out in robotics laboratories around the world.

▲ UCAVs like this will be on bomber duty by about 2015. They will gradually replace most human-crewed combat missions.

In the future, almost all combat flying will likely be carried out by UCAVs. A UCAV bomber force, like the one in the photo above left, may surround a single command plane that has a human crew onboard. The command plane will stay clear of the battle zone, while the UCAVs zoom off to attack.

ROBOFACTS: ROBOTIC MEDICAL POD TO TREAT THE INJURED

Here is an example of a plan for a robotic medical unit. Designed as a roving field hospital, a person who is far from medical facilities or medical staff, could receive treatment in an armored "pod."

These robotic pods could help people who were injured in war, or give emergency treatment to victims of natural disasters, such as earthquakes, floods, or fires.

▲ An injured soldier is taken inside a robot medical pod, where injuries are checked.

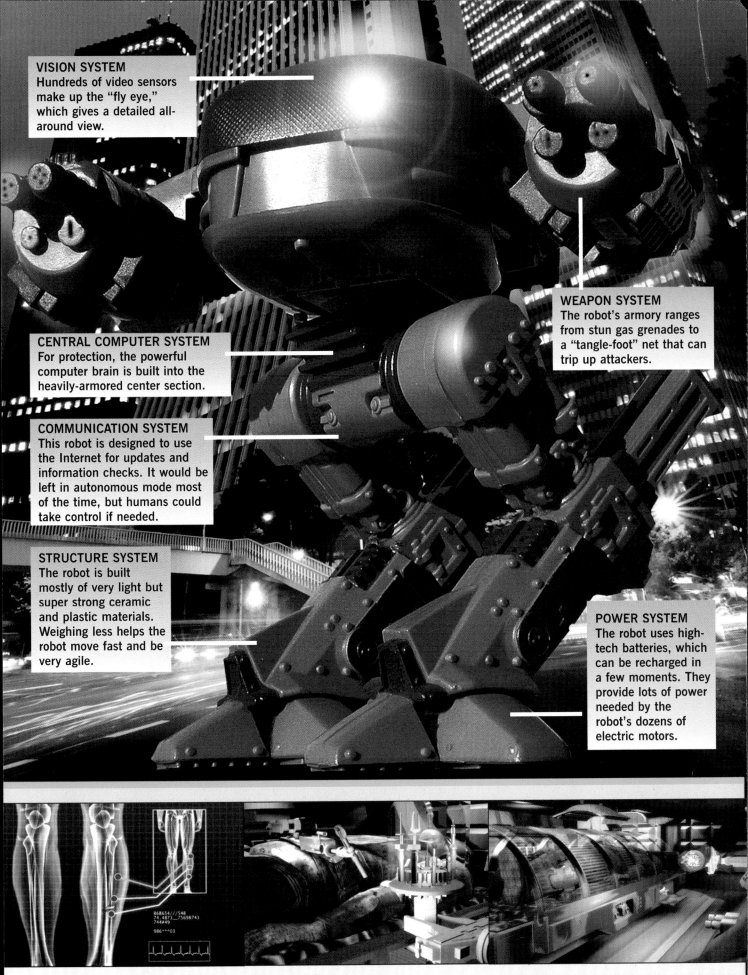

VISION SYSTEM
Hundreds of video sensors make up the "fly eye," which gives a detailed all-around view.

WEAPON SYSTEM
The robot's armory ranges from stun gas grenades to a "tangle-foot" net that can trip up attackers.

CENTRAL COMPUTER SYSTEM
For protection, the powerful computer brain is built into the heavily-armored center section.

COMMUNICATION SYSTEM
This robot is designed to use the Internet for updates and information checks. It would be left in autonomous mode most of the time, but humans could take control if needed.

STRUCTURE SYSTEM
The robot is built mostly of very light but super strong ceramic and plastic materials. Weighing less helps the robot move fast and be very agile.

POWER SYSTEM
The robot uses high-tech batteries, which can be recharged in a few moments. They provide lots of power needed by the robot's dozens of electric motors.

▲ Scanners assess leg wounds.

▲ Robots carry out emergency surgery.

▲ The soldier stays in the pod while recovering.

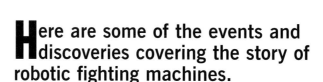

TIME TRACK

Here are some of the events and discoveries covering the story of robotic fighting machines.

▲ Leonardo da Vinci's robot knight could have looked like this if built. It is believed to be the first design for a human-shaped military robot.

▲ Security cameras help to spot suspicious packages. Here, a Wolverine police robot is tested carrying a fake briefcase bomb.

1495   Italian artist and inventor, Leonardo da Vinci (1452-1519), sketches an armored robot knight, probably the first "robot warrior." It is designed to sit up, lift its arms, and move its head. We do not know if da Vinci actually built this robot. He had many other ideas for automated weapons, including chariots and tanks.

1920   The word "robot" is used for the first time when Czech writer, Karel Capek, puts on a stage play about robots trying to take over the world. The word was coined by Capek's brother from the Czech word "robota," meaning "work."

1943   The American science fiction writer, Isaac Asimov, introduces the word "robotics" to describe the technology of robots. Through his series of stories based on a robot theme, he predicts the development of a powerful future robotics industry.

1944-5   The V-1 robotic flying bomb is used against targets in Britain and Belgium. The German weapon can fly for 150 miles (240 kilometers) at a speed of 410 miles per hour (656 kilometers per hour).

1945   The Bat guided bomb is used off the island of Borneo. It destroys several ships, including one 20 miles (32 kilometers) away.

1950s   Early computers are developed. They are very large and expensive, so are used only by governments and big corporations.

1959   The first spy satellite is launched into space by the United States. Called by the code name Corona, this space robot is the first in a long line of "Keyhole" spy satellites. More advanced satellites are being used today, which have powerful telescopes, and sensors that can see by night and day and through cloud.

1960s   Early security cameras come into use for keeping watch on traffic. Today, there are millions of these cameras. Britain is thought to be the most-watched country with more than 4 million cameras – about one for every 15 citizens.

1968   The first miniaturized computer circuit is perfected. The "**microchip**" becomes the basis of all computing machines made since, including robots.

1970s Computers start to come into general use, followed by desktop models in the 1980s. The shrinking size and price, as well as their reliability, makes computers suitable to run military robotic systems.

1972 British forces use a robot called Wheelbarrow for bomb disposal work. Ten versions of the robot have been introduced since, and they have been used many times. In 2001, a Wheelbarrow was blown clear across a London street by a terrorist bomb, but the humans working in the bomb squad were unhurt.

1982 Israel pioneers robotic military aircraft with its Scout UAV for photography, reconnaissance, and communications. UAVs have proved so useful for these purposes that dozens of different designs are now built in 18 countries.

1984 The movie *The Terminator* is released. It is a science fiction adventure story that features a traveler from the future being chased by a robot. Other movies featuring warrior robots include *Robocop* of 1987, and *Red Planet* of 2000.

1995 The Predator UCAV goes into service with the United States Air Force. Basically a UAV armed with a pair of missiles, the robot plane has been used in several countries, including Afghanistan, Bosnia, Iraq, Kosovo, and Yemen.

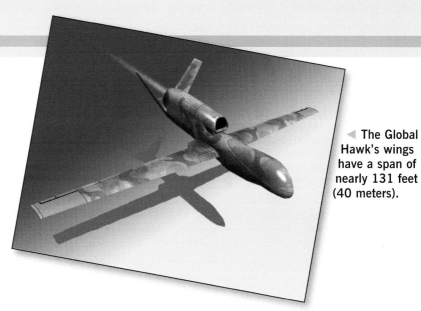

◀ The Global Hawk's wings have a span of nearly 131 feet (40 meters).

1998 First flight of the Global Hawk long-range UAV. In 2001, the robot plane makes a 22-hour non-stop flight across the Pacific Ocean from the United States to Australia, a first for an uncrewed aircraft.

2000 The Talon military robot goes into action in Bosnia. Talon is made in several different versions and can be fitted with various weapons. It is part of a plan by the United States Army to use thousands of robots in the future.

2005 Nuvo, the first in a line of smaller, simpler, and cheaper home security guard robots, goes on sale.

2006 Ofro tracked robots carry out security patrols at World Cup soccer venues across Germany. This is the first time such robots have been used at a major sports event.

2010-2015 Experts believe that many dangerous military tasks now being carried out by humans will be done by robots.

▲ Ofro security robots can patrol for up to 12 hours. Weather causes no problems because Ofro is waterproof and can work in temperatures ranging from a chilly 5°F (-15°C) to a baking 122°F (50°C).

► A technician checks the flight control system of a vertical takeoff and landing iStar UAV.

GLOSSARY

Here are explanations of many technical terms in this book.

Antenna Any aerial that is used to send or receive radio or television signals. Antennas come in many shapes and sizes – most are slim rods or round dish shapes.

Autonomous A robot that can work on its own without needing a human in control.

Carbon fiber A lightweight, yet strong material that has whiskers of carbon embedded in plastic.

Circuit Any electronic linkage that joins two or more parts together.

Computer program The set of instructions that are fed into a computer to make it work. A program is used for each separate job. For a robot, this might be a movement program or one for pattern recognition. "Software" is another word generally used for programs.

Digital The name for any device that uses the binary code for its programs, as do all computers. Binary code uses a series of ones and zeros to represent numbers and other information.

Exoskeleton Literally, an "outer skeleton," a casing that provides strength and protection.

Hydraulic system One that works by transmitting pressure along a tube or pipe through a liquid – usually water or oil.

Infrared Radiation that is given off as heat. Humans can feel infrared as warmth, though we cannot see it with our eyes. There are robot sensors that are specially designed to detect heat as easily as we see light.

Microchip The tiny, calculating part of a computer or robotic device. Microchips have taken the wires and cables of old-fashioned electronics and reduced them in size, by printing them as a circuit pattern on a small slice of silicon, known as a "chip."

Mine An explosive device that is buried under water or under the ground, just below the surface. Mines are cheap to make and to lay, and are very dangerous.

Pattern recognition A computer program that recognizes patterns from video camera pictures. Examples of such patterns could be people wearing similar clothes, or unusual behavior by one person in a large crowd.

Radar An electronic system that sends out a radio beam. Some of the beam may bounce off an object in its path, being reflected back to the transmitter. This is shown as a glowing "blip" on a video screen. Radar beams can pass through cloud, so are useful, especially in bad weather.

Radiator Also known as a "heat sink," an electronic radiator is made of thin metal surfaces that disperse a computer's heat into the surrounding air.

Reconnaissance Finding out such information as an enemy's position, movements, or weapons.

Satellite An object that orbits a larger one in space. They may be natural, such as the Moon, or artificial, like Sputnik 1, the first human-made satellite. Thousands of satellites have been launched.

Sensor The general term for any mechanical device that performs a function similar to, or often better than, human senses. Examples of robotic sensors include cameras and microphones.

Simulation Imitating the real world using a computer program. Simulations have all sorts of uses, especially for testing new design ideas before they are built, and for training purposes. Simulations save time and money. Some forms of training may be safer, too – for example, learning how to use a bomb-disposal robot.

Solar panel A flat panel made of material that converts the energy in light to electricity. Solar panels are used by many satellites as their main form of electrical power.

Swords Short for Special Weapons Observation Reconnaissance Detection Systems, part of a big robot scheme for the U.S. Army.

World War II An international war fought mostly in Europe and Asia between 1939 and 1945.

UAV, UCAV A robotic aircraft that flies without a human pilot. UAVs (Uncrewed Air Vehicles) are used mostly for spotting the enemy. UCAVs (Uncrewed Combat Air Vehicles) are robot planes that can observe the enemy and attack.

UXB Term used by bomb-disposal teams to describe the UneXploded Bombs they make safe.

V-1 An early kind of UCAV, used in World War II. It flew on a pre-set course until a timer shut off its jet engine. It then glided down to explode when it hit the ground.

▲ A Swords robot equipped with a remote-controlled gun.

▶ **A few of the many robot parts and self-assembly kits on sale.**

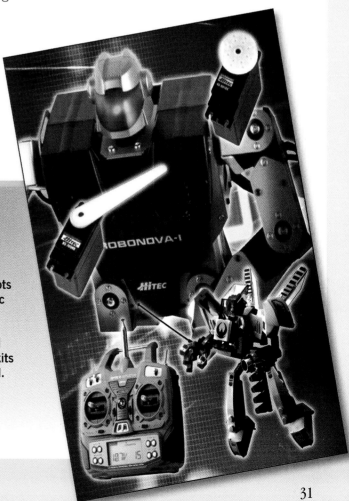

ROBOZONES: NEXT STEPS

Robotics is an area of science that has been forecast in many ways by the writers of science fiction. Many science fiction stories have explored how robots might be developed, and the ways they could affect people.

If you would like to read stories about robots, the works of American writer Isaac Asimov make a good start. Many other science fiction writers have written about robots.

The movies mentioned in this book also make interesting statements about robots.

Another way to explore robots is to try building one. Electronic stores and Internet sites sell a range of robot parts, from a dazzling collection of individual components, to self-assembly kits that have all the parts included.

INDEX

Acknowledgements
We wish to thank all those individuals
and organizations that have helped to
create this publication. Information and
images were supplied by:
Alpha Archive, BAe Systems, Berkeley
Robotics Laboratory, Boeing Corp,
Boston Dynamics, Tony Bostrom
Perceptive Designs, DARPA Defense
Advanced Research Agency, Foster-
Miller Inc, Fotolia, Fraunhofer Institute,
General Atomics Aeronautical Systems,
Hitec Robotics, Hylands Underwater
Vehicles, iRobot Corp, iStockphoto,
David Jefferis, NASA Space Agency,
Northeastern University, Northrop
Grumman Corp, Octatron Inc, Office of
Naval Research, Pacific Western
Lightstorm Entertainment, Remotec Inc,
Saab Aerosystems, Sandia National
Laboratories, Sanyo Electric Co, SRI
International, tmsuk Co Ltd, U.S. Army,
Navy, and Air Force, Village Roadshow
Pictures/Warner Bros, ZMP Inc.

Printed in the U.S.A.